What's So Funny?

How to Sharpen Your Sense of Humor

by Paul Moran

WHAT'S SO FUNNY?

HOW TO SHARPEN YOUR SENSE OF HUMOR.

ISBN 978-1-4303-0114-1

Published by LuLu Enterprises, Inc.

(www.lulu.com)

Dedicated to Linda

Laugh – the general word for the sounds or exhalation made in expressing mirth amusement, etc. Chuckle, giggle, titter, snicker, snigger, guffaw, chortle, cackle, roar, snort, crow, shriek, howl.

Webster's New World Dictionary

Preface

Books about comedy are usually amusing, and I hope this one is no exception, but that's not why I wrote it. <u>What's So Funny?</u> is not a joke book, a how-to book for stand-up comedians, a dictionary of amusing anecdotes, or a guide to one-liners for public speakers. Professional comics and humor writers more experienced than myself have already written those books.

My aim is different. I want to help you sharpen your sense of humor by showing you how to think funny every day, wherever you go, any time you choose. It may seem natural to "get serious" and rely upon logical thinking whenever you're confronted with a difficult problem, but sometimes sharing a good laugh is a more effective way to discover a solution, reveal a hidden truth, or revive an optimistic outlook.

My own interest in humor grew from years of teaching middle school students who didn't, couldn't or wouldn't fit into the mainstream of school life. The school system called them "special", and indeed they were. Most everything about them was a surprise, and our time together often seemed like the punch line in a running gag.

Some students hadn't yet mastered basic skills like reading or simple mathematics, but managed to excel when it came to activities like repairing home appliances, playing heavy metal music on an electric guitar, or memorizing the weekly television schedule.

One boy couldn't remember which class to go to next, but never missed the nightly news and gave us detailed reports on political events in the Middle East. Another was a poor speller and could barely read, but carried around the official Star Trek Klingon dictionary and impressed us by writing notes in Klingon and speaking the language fluently, or as near as anyone could tell.

We used standard textbooks nearly every day, but I also created additional offbeat teaching materials, decorated the classroom with cartoons, taught simple magic tricks, and handed out silly prizes. Oftentimes I'd praise students for making their best efforts, only to see them penalized in other classes for not performing as well as their peers on standardized tests and assignments.

I never knew what to expect next, and I often wondered how any of it was possible. Still, hardly a day went by without laughter, and humor seemed to help get us through the waves of frustration and discouragement. It also contributed to more positive attitudes, greater understanding and increased learning. You might say that laughter set in motion a paradigm shift in the classroom from self-doubt to self-confidence.

Eventually I included comedy as an official topic of study, and that was when I saw how quickly anyone could learn to think funny.

Paul Moran
Fairfax, VA.
2006

What's So Funny?

How to Sharpen Your Sense of Humor

TABLE OF CONTENTS

Introduction

Whatever makes you laugh is funny, and anything is funny if it makes you laugh. That is the basic truth about humor. Ridiculous events are happening everywhere, every day. Turn on your television. Pick up a newspaper. Surf the net. Look out your window. The opportunities to laugh are enormous even for the most sober-minded among us.

So, when was the last time <u>you</u> laughed out loud? I'm not talking about giggles or chuckles, but real guffaws. Has it been longer than a day or two? Well then, perhaps your sense of humor could use a little sharpening. If so, this book is for you. If not, this book is for somebody else. But please, read it anyway. It's about adding humor to your life, questioning the status quo, and noticing the difference between the way things are and the way they could be. It's also about putting a smile on your face, a laugh in your belly, and learning how to make a fool of yourself.

And, there's more! I've also included a bit of philosophy for those intent on taking themselves seriously, and plenty of synonyms for readers looking to improve their vocabulary. (Why settle for saying something one way, when there are ten additional ways to say the same thing?)

Most importantly, I've described a number of simple techniques anyone can use to sharpen his or her sense of humor and generate some laughter and good feelings.

So, go ahead. Enjoy yourself.

*There's a lot to be said for making people
laugh. Did you know that's all some people
have? It isn't much, but it's better than nothing
in this cockeyed caravan.*
Preston Sturges: Sullivan's Travels (1941)

Life, Death, Laughs

We humans are a funny bunch of mammals. We're physical beings whose main survival tool is mental. Though it's not always obvious, we use our brainpower to define and solve problems with the hope of creating some kind of order out of the chaos. Then, just when we think we've got life completely under control, something unexpected happens to remind us we're not entirely in charge. Such unforeseen events sometimes make us laugh, and when they do the days seem more enjoyable.

Whether you think you're funny or not, you must admit that laughter feels good. The funny side of the street is a great place to take a stroll, and you'll find it wherever you go because the jokes are always on us.

We are all alive, yet as physical beings we eventually die. So here's the basic question: What's to be done in the meantime? How you respond to that question is an individual matter, but there's no denying being alive is one experience we all share. I suggest we celebrate that fact and enjoy it together with humor.

You Are Funny

Is a keen sense of humor something only a select few are born with, or can it be developed by anyone?

The answers to these questions are: Yes and Yes. We've all met people who seem to get a laugh no matter what they say or do. Ask professional comedians what led them into a career in comedy, and many will tell you they were simply born to be funny. If it's true that some people are funnier than others, how they came to be that way is ultimately irrelevant. If you have ever laughed, you have a sense of humor. So why can't you also learn to think funny, be funny and look at the world from a comic point of view?

What makes you laugh? A stand-up comedian, TV sitcoms, clowns? How about editorial cartoons, magicians, feature films, ventriloquists, and impressionists? Perhaps it's your Uncle Ed's antics at the dinner table, the way your best friend mispronounces words, or your face in the mirror when you wake up in the morning. Any situation has its funny side if you know where to look for it. But what makes one situation funnier than another?

Much of what's funny involves a shared experience, something unexpected, and the element of surprise. Let's say you're standing on a corner in your hometown, when suddenly a policeman in uniform marches down the middle of Main Street walking a flock of chickens, each one on a leash. That's unexpected, surprising, and likely to make you laugh. Ha, ha, ha. Ho, ho, ho. The sight of the policeman with the chickens has brightened your day, and it would be even more fun if you could share it with someone. Sharing the laughter enriches the experience by confirming your own good feelings and spreading the joy around. Since shared laughter has this added value, I'll be emphasizing it throughout the rest of this book.

A note of caution: Nervous laughter is not much fun. If you plan to amuse people by making them extremely uncomfortable and anxious, then you also need to let them know they are safe or they won't stick around to hear what you have to say. Part of your job as the funny person is to let others know you're there to share a good time. If they expect to laugh and you can somehow surprise them, you'll have a decent chance of being funny. This is true even if your approach is threatening, outrageous and seems insulting. Go ahead and take your audience to the edge of the comedy cliff, but don't just shock them or they may leave angry instead of amused.

We humans are social animals, and we like to be entertained. It makes us happy and provides a welcome respite the more mundane aspects of life such as food gathering, paying the mortgage, and maintaining our oh-so-youthful appearances. Any audience (friends, co-workers, or captives) naturally expects to enjoy themselves. They're waiting to hear your story, read your writing, or view your work, and they're prepared to consider whatever you have to offer. Their minds are open, and they'll suspend judgment at least for a while. Now, how will you make them laugh?

The whole object of comedy is to be yourself and the closer you get to that, the funnier you will be.

Jerry Seinfeld

Surprise

How often have you told a funny story only to get to the end and realize that, well, I guess you had to be there? The story was surprising, unexpected and funny to you, but somehow your friends did not share your enthusiasm. There could be many reasons why they didn't laugh: Maybe you mixed up the order of events, left out important details, or failed to pay your share of the bar tab. The most likely reason is they simply were not surprised.

Almost every funny situation involves a surprise of some kind. "But", you say, " I already expect to laugh whenever I tune in to a sitcom, visit a comedy club, or dine with my Uncle Ed. Where's the surprise in that?"

Sure, you're inclined to laugh, hoping to laugh, maybe even expecting to laugh, but you won't let out a real guffaw unless you're surprised. Despite being predictable, TV sitcoms are structured in ways that set you up for laughter. You may think you know what's coming, but you can't be certain until it actually arrives. Punch lines are meant to do just that; deliver a surprise punch that makes you bend over with laughter. Even the most worn out jokes can elicit a chuckle or a groan, as you'll see later.

Surprise is nothing more than experiencing the unexpected. So before you can create a surprise and perhaps a few laughs, you'll need to have a good idea of what is expected. Even though human perception is uniquely individual and we each must work out our own personal view of what life is all about, people are still more alike than different. It's this recognition of what we have in common that allows the members of the human race to live in such blissful peace and harmony with each other.

Okay, so there are a few remaining social, economic and political issues we need to resolve, but that doesn't alter the fact that we really do have a lot in common with each other. Therefore, one of the best ways to understand someone else's expectations is to examine your own. Consider this situation:

Sunbathers watch a man in a bathing suit walk along the beach.

Average, normal sunbathers spending an average, normal day at the beach. Where's the surprise in that?

No matter how ordinary the circumstance, there is always some aspect that stands out, something that makes any particular situation different from all others. That's because there is no such thing as "average, normal sunbathers", an "average, normal day at the beach", or an average, normal anything. "Average" and "normal" are simply generalities. So as the sunbathers in our example watch a man in a bathing suit walk along the beach, what specifically might you notice first? Sex appeal aside for the moment, what might draw your attention?

Well, it could be something obvious such as the man's physical appearance. Maybe he's extremely thin, fat, tall, or short. Or, perhaps it's the color, size or shape of his swimsuit. But it might be something else like the weather conditions, the surf, or the reactions of the sunbathers. Whatever it is, that's your starting point. You noticed something specific. It grabbed your attention, and now you've got the raw material to create something unexpected, surprising and perhaps funny.

Divergent Thinking

Divergent thinking is simply thinking in a new direction; thinking in ways that deviate from the norm. Here's how you can use it to generate possible surprises. Rather than accepting a situation as it is, try to upset, reject, or oppose it. Ask yourself, "What if conditions were radically different?" Try to imagine the opposite or reverse of the situation, and don't be afraid to embellish the details. Exercise your sense of the absurd and remember you're a humorist looking to create a surprise, not a detective in search of the facts.

Taking our example, let's say what stands out most is the sunbathers doing the watching. There they sit in their sunglasses and floppy hats. What we'd expect is that they can easily see the man in the bathing suit as he walks along the beach.

But what if the opposite is true? What if they cannot see him? What if their view is suddenly obstructed? Or, what if, unbeknownst to the man in the bathing suit, they are all blind? The onlookers cannot see him, yet he believes he has their full attention.

Now, what if our man is the type who craves the spotlight? Perhaps he fancies himself an athlete or body-builder. Can you picture this?

Blind sunbathers sit passively in their sunglasses and floppy hats, as a bodybuilder poses and performs assorted feats of strength at the water's edge.

Notice how everything grows out of the original idea, and depends upon it to generate an unexpected surprise. A body-builder posing for blind sunbathers is only surprising because it is no longer what we expected, namely: Sunbathers watch a man in a bathing suit walk along the beach.

Chaos in the midst of chaos isn't funny,
but chaos in the midst of order is.
Steve Martin

More Surprises

Let's take our example in some other directions. Again think in terms of reversing the situation, or opposing the action, and use your imagination to add supporting details. For example: How might the sunbathers, the beach, the man or his bathing suit, be turned into contradictory, contrasting, incompatible, antithetical, or even antagonistic elements? Simply put, and without all those synonyms: Take what you started with and create something radically different.

Here are some possibilities:

Reversal: Let's reverse the action by turning the observers into the observed. Now it's the man who closely inspects the sunbathers through giant binoculars as he walks along the edge of the water.

Opposite: We can turn the interested sunbathers into their opposite: indifferent bystanders. No longer curious onlookers, they are bored and openly ignore the muscle-flexing man in the tiny bathing suit.

Contradictory: Let's turn the tables on our attention-seeking man in a bathing suit by having him suddenly confronted by nude sunbathers. Here he sets out to impress everyone with his physique, and instead he is the one who is shocked and embarrassed. He expected compliments, but ends up being ridiculed for his inappropriate attire.

Contrasting: Why not have our characters react differently, and unexpectedly, to the same environment? Maybe it's windy and our sunbathers are cold and shivering. Let's wrap them in blankets, and huddle them together for warmth. There, that's better. But, wait! What do they see? Why it's a man dressed in a Speedo confidently striding through the waves along the shore. He must be freezing. Why is he waving and smiling? The same conditions; different reactions.

Incompatible: What's wrong with this picture? Sunbathers stare at a man in a tuxedo as he nimbly sidesteps the crashing waves. Sand plus water plus a tuxedo, equals one strange and surprising combination.

Antithetical: Bikini-clad sunbathers slather on the suntan lotion as they sit safely in the shade of their umbrellas, while a fully-clothed man floats on a raft in order to better soak up the sun's ultraviolet rays. These characters are working against themselves. The sunbathers avoid the sun by sitting in the shade, and the man can't get a tan because his skin is completely covered.

Antagonistic: Sunbathers uniformly dressed in red shorts and tee-shirts patrol the perimeter of a giant sand castle, and refuse passage to a man dressed in blue. The scene could turn hostile, and perhaps humorous, if the sunbathers try to enforce their nonsensical standards of beach behavior.

Once again, notice how each example flows from the original idea. Take a moment now and ask yourself how you might turn it into something else that's surprisingly different. You might try adding dissimilar, unsuitable, or incongruous elements – anything that seems out of place – to the situation.

You can observe a lot just by watching.
Yogi Berra

The FID Factors

The FID Factors refer to the Frequency, Intensity, and Duration of an activity. Eating, sleeping, staring at a cup of coffee as it slowly revolves inside a microwave oven, in fact any activity can be described in terms of its frequency (how often it occurs), intensity (how much force is applied), and duration (how much time it takes). One way to develop new ideas is to ask yourself how a situation might change if you adjusted one or more of the FID Factors.

Frequency: How often does our man walk along the beach? Once a day? Once a year? Every hour on the hour?

Intensity: Does he vigorously march across the sand, or is he a plodder?

Duration: Has he been walking for five minutes, five hours or five days?

The FID Factors can help you look closely at a specific activity, and consider it in extreme terms. How much is too much? How little is too little? It doesn't matter to what degree you alter any one or all three FID Factors, as long as you generate a surprise. If you can do that, you will have a good chance of producing some laughter.

This is a good place to point out that a surprise by itself will not <u>guarantee</u> laughter. In fact there is no way to predict when or if your listeners, readers or viewers will ever laugh out loud. After all, that's up to them. Whether something is funny or not will depend upon their particular sensibilities, but there are definite techniques you can use to sharpen your own sense of humor and improve the odds. One of the most useful is exaggeration.

Those who can't laugh at themselves
leave the job to others.
Anonymous

More Is Better

If you've ever told stories about your romantic adventures, you know how to exaggerate. Exaggeration stretches an experience to the edges of believability and turns it into something unexpected. Exaggeration – making more of something than its reality would dictate – is a matter of degree, with trivial embellishment at one end (We kissed on the lips – twice!) and shameless outrageousness at the other (We kissed on the lips until they went numb and we collapsed from lack of oxygen, and fire fighters arrived and had to use the Jaws of Life to separate us, but we wouldn't let them, so then…!).

Exaggeration is most effective when it's used to create contrast, or to highlight something such as your attitude, perceptions, or feelings. By widening the gap between everyone else's sense of reality and your own, you may produce an unexpected surprise.

There are plenty of ways to exaggerate, or overdo it. Here are a variety of examples which, like all those in this book, are included for illustrative purposes only. Why not take the time to create a few of your own? Practice, as you'll soon discover, is the quickest way to sharpen your sense of humor.

Overstate: Try making a fuss over something small or insignificant. Turn a minor inconvenience into a major confrontation, or provide an endless stream of details about an inconsequential event. You could also place too much importance upon an event like this one.

I got a letter from our local Public Television station.

They've asked me to become a dues-paying member.

Can you believe it? They selected me!

Magnify: Try to adopt a lopsided point of view. Make something greater in size, status or importance than might be expected. Or, you might want to exaggerate by turning a molehill into a mountain.

Who left that unattended vehicle in front of my

lovely home? Why, it hasn't even been washed!

It should be ticketed and towed. Furthermore, I

demand the arrest of its owner on charges of littering,

trespassing, and assault with an ugly automobile!

Enlarge: Expound upon seemingly significant connections between unrelated items or events. Widen the boundaries of an event's importance, such as this item found in a tourist guidebook.

Must See! The Original Tucker Family Kitchen Table. Site of the first Tucker Family Checkers Tournament probably held during July of 1956. Contestants included Mr. Tom Tucker, Mrs. Tammy Tucker, and their son Timmy. Visitors may view official tournament records scribbled on a nearby wall. Allow six minutes for the tour. Tickets: $17.50.

Overemphasize: Belabor a point. Dwell on a subject until you've run it into the ground. Explain it in extreme detail. Choosing an insignificant topic like this one can help.

Trimming with scissors may be the number one cause of lost toenail clippings. The slicing action of the scissor blades places an intense downward pressure on the nail, which in turn hurls the unwanted edges into the air. I've clocked some clippings at speeds nearing ninety-three miles per hour, and many travel up to thirty-two feet before landing.

Intensify: Increase the force of your presentation. Heighten your emotions. Let yourself become angry or aggravated about your topic even if it's implausible.

I dare anyone to spend a day with the maliciously monstrous mice roaming my kitchen! Yesterday one ripped the door off my refrigerator searching for cheese, then held a butter knife to my throat and demanded I fill his satchel with Kraft Single Slices. Oh, he tried to scurry away, but I got a good look at him. I'd recognize that scruffy gray coat and those beady little eyes anywhere.

Amplify: Develop your topic more fully by providing details or specific examples. Here, we're invited to examine the fine print.

I must protest the final results of the pie eating contest.

The fine print on page two-hundred and seventy-four

of the Official Pie Eater's Rule Book clearly says:

"All fruit pies shall be covered with a light crisscross

crust." Nevertheless, I was forced to devour an entire

cherry pie topped with an unseemly thick whole wheat

crust and gigantic fluted edges!

Elaborate: Make the situation more complicated. Use real or imaginary details to embellish the facts. You might even invent a story like this.

Too many young children run loose in my

neighborhood, so I fired up the old VW Bus and

together we rounded up a herd of thirty or forty head.

They'll be grazing in my basement for the next few

days before I auction them off at the next block party.

Got me a set of triplets should fetch top dollar.

Overestimate: Place too high a value on something, or give it too much importance. Misjudge or misunderstand an obvious set of circumstances as if you were blinded by love.

I sneezed, and she actually glanced in my direction. She tilted her head about three inches, and I swear we made eye contact. There was definitely left-eye contact and probably right-eye contact as well, although it was hard to tell because she quickly covered her face with her hands. It must be love!

Sensationalize: Use extreme descriptions that shock, startle, amaze or thrill. You might even try threatening physical harm to yourself or others, or violating social rules of conduct with insults or angry outbursts. Sometimes what's left to the imagination can also be outrageous.

I agree stray cats are a problem, but there's good news too. It only took one to feed my entire family.

Exaggeration can also simplify your message. Use it to focus your audience's attention, especially if you want them to consider an extreme or uncomfortable point of view. Note how this example challenges our assumptions about violence.

Sure I've chopped onions. I've chopped them into teeny-tiny bits for hours without shedding a single tear, and I've smiled from ear to ear as I plunged dozens of baby carrots into a giant pot of boiling water. Why, I've even laughed out loud as I cracked open a fresh head of lettuce with a hammer and chisel. So what! Is it a crime to hate vegetables?

Overstate, magnify, enlarge, overemphasize, intensify, amplify, elaborate, overestimate, or sensationalize. The method and the terminology don't matter as long as you remember that effective exaggeration moves beyond the limits of what's expected.

Normal is in the eye of the beholder.
Whoopi Goldberg

31

Make It Trivial

Exaggeration challenges normal behavior by going beyond its limits, but you can also think funny by heading in the opposite direction. Use understatement – the art of minimizing – to trivialize something.

An easy way to get started is to choose a serious topic you consider controversial or important to yourself or your audience. The more deeply held the belief, the more easily it can be undermined. It could be anything from local prejudices about the weather to the spread of nuclear weapons throughout the world. Pick one you feel strongly about. Like this one:

The death penalty should be repealed.

Now identify some reasons to support your opinion.

Killing people is barbaric.

Innocent people are being executed by mistake.

Criminals should be rehabilitated.

Choose one of these to work with, and try to trivialize it. Here are some examples.

Express apathy: *Innocent people are being executed by mistake.* Oh well, c'est la vie.

Overlook important details: *Innocent people are being executed by mistake.* Sure, but I hear that prison food is darn tasty.

Underestimate: *Innocent people are being executed by mistake.* At least they won't have to spend the rest of their lives in prison.

Make light of the details: *Innocent people are being executed by mistake.* Yes, but everybody makes mistakes.

Shrinking: *Innocent people are being executed by mistake.* Those aren't mistakes. They're minor lapses in judgment.

Be unaware: *Innocent people are being executed by mistake?* Really? Nobody mentioned that at the going-away party last night.

Express tedium: *Innocent people are being executed by mistake.* If I've heard that once, I've heard it a thousand times. Enough about "innocent people" already!

Appear bored: You can easily undercut the importance of an idea by appearing uninterested, listless, dull or complacent as you discuss it.

Understatement also works with everyday events. Pick out something obvious, and minimize or ignore it.

Consider our example of the man walking the beach. Here he is again walking along posing and flexing, and dressed only in the skimpiest of bathing suits. One of the onlookers might say to the others, "He's going to regret not wearing a hat in this hot sun."

Notice how understatement actually focuses our attention on the obvious fact that the man is prancing around nearly naked. The onlookers are sharing a secret joke. It's clear the man wants them to notice his body, and they cannot help but do so. Yet instead of giving him that satisfaction, they undermine his intentions by emphasizing the most trivial detail: his bare head. Their response is a surprise to him, and to us. It may even be funny.

I've had great success being a total idiot.

Jerry Lewis

Classic Joke Structure

Surprises can come from any direction, and sometimes the most hilarious situations result from the most outrageous events. An audience laughs when they realize how mistaken they have been in their thinking. Suddenly the surprise makes sense, just not the kind of sense they expected.

An easy way to prepare your readers, viewers or listeners to laugh is to clearly define their expectations. This part of a typical joke is usually called the set-up. The classic joke structure involves a set-up line, followed by a second set-up line, followed by the punch line. The effect is similar to a magician's use of misdirection; while you're busy looking one way the magic is taking place somewhere else.

The initial set-up introduces the topic and helps the audience feel secure in its understanding of the situation.

The second set-up reinforces or validates the first. It establishes a pattern. This may be done through simple repetition.

Once the audience starts to feel secure and confident, once they believe they know what to expect next, they are surprised by the punch line.

You're essentially telling the audience: "Here's exactly what you can expect. Let me tell you again: Here's what to expect. Feel comfortable? Good. SURPRISE! Ha! Ha! Ha!" The surprise element, the punch line, comes just as the audience begins to draw its own conclusions from the set-up lines. Suddenly they realize they've been fooled, and they laugh at the their own folly.

Some writers call this three-part structure The Rule Of Threes, and believe it is actually hard-wired into our brains. It certainly is a convenient and efficient method if you want to be funny, whether telling a story, writing an essay, drawing a cartoon, or editing a film. Take a close look at this well-worn example:

A three-legged dog walks into a saloon, orders a
drink, and says to the bartender: "I'm lookin'
for the man that shot my paw."

Set-up:

The audience is immediately asked to accept the premise that a three-legged dog can walk. The word "saloon" triggers several associations. We can easily imagine the dog walking upright and swinging open those wooden saloon doors. The setting is most likely the Old West, and the dog is probably male since respectable women didn't enter saloons in those days.

Reinforcing Set-up:

The dog orders a drink, so he is also a talking dog. We readily accept this because we have already allowed the dog to walk into a saloon, and it's not much of a stretch to believe he can also talk.

Next he orders a drink. Can you see him leaning against the bar in classic western fashion? He may even wear chaps, a holster, boots and a ten-gallon hat. So, this dog is standing by himself at the bar and is being served a drink. Perhaps he's a stranger in town. Such loners often make inquiries of bartenders. Now, what might he say?

Punch line:

"I'm lookin' (not looking, but the western lookin') for the man that shot my paw." The word 'shot' indicates, as in most film westerns we've seen, gunplay is involved. Now the picture becomes clear. This lone dog is after revenge, and it's definitely a family affair because he wants to find the man that shot his father – his "paw".

Note that the funny twist, the surprise, the punch comes at the absolute end. "Paw" is the last word we hear. And, if we were truly in the Old West, we'd pronounce the word "paw" instead of "pa".

The funny aspect of this classic joke is a simple word play, a pun. Recall the beginning of the joke: the dog is a three-legged dog. He's <u>literally</u> missing his paw. We've been had. We went along with the idea of a talking three-legged dog, and now we've been led down the punster's path. The joke's on us!

If you want to create a joke that packs a strong punch, keep it simple and be specific. Each word in this example is important. The audience's train of thought travels down a single track until they are hit with the punch line. There are no side trips, extraneous details, sweeping generalities or flowery descriptions, which might lead them away from their ultimate destination. The audience thinks they understand completely. They mistakenly believe they can anticipate what will happen next, and it's at that moment they are surprised by the punch line.

When people are laughing, they're generally
not killing one another.
Alan Alda

Groups Of Threes

Here's an easy way to generate a laugh. Start looking around and you'll see groups of threes here (1), there (2) and everywhere (3):

Stories have three parts: a beginning, a middle and an end.

Nursery rhymes are full of threes: the three little pigs, the three bears, and the three blind mice.

The Olympics awards three medals in every event including the triple jump, also called the hop, skip and jump.

Popular phrases also come in threes like beg, borrow or steal; cool, calm and collected; or eat, drink and be merry.

And don't forget three meals a day, the 3Rs, three ring circuses, and The Three Stooges.

Groups of threes are used everywhere. Audiences are accustomed to hearing them and will anticipate their meaning.

It follows that any group of three carries with it powerful audience expectations. You can use this fact to your advantage.

Changing any one of the items in a group of three will surprise your audience, but you'll generate more laughs if you stick with the classic joke structure.

Let the first two items in the group become your setups, and then replace the third item with a punch line.

A lucky poker player might advise his fellow gamblers to beg, borrow or deal.

An elite private school might teach reading, writing, and real estate.

What if Goldilocks met Papa Bear, Mamma Bear, and Cousin Bubba Bear?

Finding groups of threes can become addictive once you get started, so why not develop a humor habit and enjoy creating those punch lines?

Defining Expectations

Expectations are built upon past experiences. We expect certain things to happen because we've experienced something like them before. Given a situation, we anticipate a set of possible outcomes; what might conceivably happen. There are any number of possibilities of course, but daily living has taught us to depend upon what we've already learned.

Audiences also have a set of experiences and expectations, so the better you know your audience the easier it will be to lead them to laughter. Your presentation need not make sense immediately, but it must be recognizable or at least tolerable. You can be a lunatic, fool, critic, or clown, even present the absurd, as long as your audience can recognize it for what it is: absurd. If what you have to offer simply leaves them confused, you'll have defeated your own purpose.

So here's a twist: Why not give your audience exactly what it expects? That may seem to go against all that's been said so far about creating surprises, but sometimes people don't realize what they expect and you can generate a surprise, and some laughter, simply by pointing out the obvious.

Let's say your Uncle Ed loves to talk about the weather. He's been doing it for years, and now the entire family takes it for granted that Uncle Ed will provide them with the latest local forecast whenever and wherever they see him. The family accepts it and expects it, but do they realize how funny Uncle Ed's behavior might look to the rest of the world? Why not provide them with some humorous hypotheticals?

Picture Uncle Ed at the doctor's office: "I've got this pain in my shoulder that started Wednesday afternoon. The sky was partly cloudy and there was a slight chance of showers. The high temperature for the day hit eighty-six degrees, which set a new record for the month of May...."

At a wedding: "Congratulations to both of you on this overcast morning with a sixty-percent chance of precipitation. I hope you enjoy your honeymoon in Miami Beach, but there's a tropical depression forming along the coast and it's gaining strength as a cold front moves in from the north...."

Or, on the witness stand: "Yes, I remember seeing the defendant at the scene of the crime. Her brown hair was blowing from the northeast at ten miles per hour with gusts between thirty and thirty-five, and she was carrying an umbrella even though the forecast called for clear skies...."

Notice how exaggeration highlights the behavior everyone takes for granted, and creates a recognizable surprise. The result is often laughter.

Doubt is not a pleasant condition, but
certainty is absurd.
Voltaire

Logical Delusions

Reason tells us the world operates according to a logical set of understandable rules. Eventually everything we experience can be categorized and logically explained. Humor, on the other hand, tells us the world is simultaneously rational and ridiculous; sensible and irrational. It explains reality by revealing the incongruous and often inexplicable aspects of human experience.

Furthermore, reason and humor tend to neutralize each other. Try to rationally explain a joke to someone and you'll soon discover it's no longer as funny as it was a moment ago. Likewise, mockery can often render useless even the most persuasive logical argument.

Humorists realize no matter how hard we try to make sense of life, it is just too mysterious, varied and full of change to be pinned down by reason alone. It's foolish to divide the world into black and white while ignoring the gray areas, or to establish a strict set of rules without accounting for possible exceptions. That's why following a narrow line of thinking to its logical conclusion is often absurd, and sometimes funny.

Dogmatists, bigots and zealots are easy targets for humorists, but you can be just as funny exposing the common everyday brand of human single-mindedness. Stretch any belief or principle far enough, and you can usually expose its absurdity. Your audience will be surprised to find out how silly we humans sometimes behave. Done well, the overall effect is self-mockery; one of the most likable types of humor. Here's how to get started.

1.   Pick an activity, set of beliefs or an opinion.

2.   Identify the essential reasoning behind it.

3.   Ask what might happen if it were carried out to its ultimate, logical conclusion.

It helps to think in absolute terms like: never, always, forever, final, permanently, at the limit, everybody, nobody, all or none. For example, here's a curiously common behavior:

Anyone who owns a dining room table worries about scratching, denting, or discoloring its finish. Many owners will go to great lengths to protect its appearance.

Rationale behind the behavior:

Dining room tables are expensive, and must be
be protected from accidental damage.

Now take this belief to its logical conclusion by
thinking in absolutes:

Is it *ever* okay to eat at the dining room table?

If the dining room table must *never* be used,
then where and how will we eat?

Can the table be protected *permanently*?

Let's consider this last question. Can you develop an
answer that makes logical sense, but takes it to extremes?

Here's one possibility extended to its seemingly
inevitable conclusion. Notice how the actions sound
reasonable at first, but then escalate into the absurd.

To permanently protect your dining room table: First, coat the table with a fine furniture wax. Then, cover the waxed finish with a linen tablecloth. Next, protect the tablecloth with a thick sheet of glass. To shield the glass from scratches and spills, top it with a sheet of plastic. Over that goes a second tablecloth to conceal the plastic. To protect the second tablecloth purchase a set of matching linen place mats, and cover them with plastic wrap. If eating becomes absolutely necessary, hand out plastic utensils, paper plates, and disposable rubber gloves (to eliminate fingerprints).

Protect the table at any cost. The wood needs protection so it's given a wax finish. But now the wax must be protected, so it's covered with a tablecloth, and on and on. Eventually the finish of the dining room table is completely hidden, yet it is also *permanently* protected. Sound logical?

It's this type of fractured reasoning you want an audience to pick up on. They'll be surprised at how logical it seems, and that's what makes it potentially funny. It all makes a certain kind of sense, nobody wants to damage an expensive dining room table, but the final result is absurd.

Your Powerful Brain

Here's a quick exercise designed to generate new comic ideas. Make two lists of items. You can use anything that pops into your head. The more unusual, the better. The number of items doesn't matter.

Next, randomly link any item from the first list with any item from the second. This will create some unexpected combinations, which is exactly what you want. Almost immediately, your powerful brain will begin making connections between the two. Why? Because, that's what brains do. Just let it go to work, while you record the results.

Now look over your new ideas. Some will make sense. Some will be nonsense. A few might strike you funny. If you're not satisfied with your first attempt, try linking two other ideas or add more items to your lists. Here's an example:

List A	List B
trophy	propellers
barbecue sauce	pencil sharpener
photography	running a race
jungle cats	slippers

I'll randomly link "trophy" and "slippers". Here are my immediate connections:

1. Accepting an award dressed in my slippers.
2. The Gold Slipper Award.
3. Trophy for sleeping on the couch.
4. Woman in pajamas putting on a pair of slippers.
5. 'Slippers' is the name of an ice hockey team.

Some of these seem closely related to each other, but I like the idea of a Gold Slipper Award the best. Who would receive such an award, and why? It sounds somewhat funny already, so it's the one I'll ask my powerful brain to work on.

I'm imagining a pair of golden slippers being presented on stage to a woman in pajamas. What stands out is the award, so I'll try to exaggerate it.

What if the Gold Slipper Award is a pair of three-foot long, solid gold slippers? Two or three men carry them onto the stage and place them on the winner's feet. She's a woman in a shabby bathrobe who just woke up. The slippers are so heavy she can barely walk. A speaker announces the winner's name, and a well-dressed audience stands and cheers. The winner waves and blows kisses as she slowly shuffles off stage.

You can use this exercise in a variety of ways:

- Narrow individual topics by assigning one to list A and one to list B. Use free association to brainstorm five to ten specific ideas for each topic, and then randomly combine the two lists. Use the results as a starting point to think funny.

Visiting the Dentist	Playing Poker
teeth cleaned	cards
fillings	poker chips
drill	raising the bid
smiling dentist	winning hand
dental floss	aces

Teeth cleaned combined with *raising the bid:*
What if dentists only offered their services to the highest bidders? Maybe five or six patients are given the same appointment. They bid on services like cleaning, root canals, and crowns. Winning bidders get their teeth fixed. Losers wait until the next appointment when more patients arrive to join the auction. What might eventually happen?

- Focus even more specifically on a single subject. Identify ten or more items related to your topic. Separate those items into two lists, and then randomly combine them. This is a good way to generate ideas for a humorous speech or essay.

Joe Smith's Retirement

He worked here for thirty years	Joe still looks young
Has five children	Needs a new car
Wife continues to work	Never gets sick
Joe likes to travel	Who will replace Joe?

- Set up your lists to explore strong feelings: likes, dislikes, fears, attractions, etc. Some professional comedians claim the world of extreme emotions is the best place to get material. Use free association – any responses are acceptable – and let your powerful brain uncover the connections.

One doesn't have a sense of humor.
It has you.
Larry Gelbart

What's Really Going On?

If you sat quietly staring at a bound bundle of printed papers held in front of you, and then regularly turned individual pages, I'd say you were probably reading because that's what reading looks like. What we call reading ultimately refers to a collection of specific behaviors, just like any other idea. Sometimes we can forget that fact and act as if we lived in a world of ideas. Whenever that happens, whenever real world behaviors are ignored, taken for granted or hidden under a heavy blanket of generalities, you have an opportunity to generate laughter. How? By pointing out the obvious.

Pretend you are a scientific observer, or the proverbial visitor from another planet, pick some typical human activity or idea and then try to define it by describing the behaviors you notice in literal terms.

A football game: A mob of oversize men dressed in tights, giant plastic headgear, and foam rubber padding, bang heads and jump on each other while chasing after an inflated pig's skin.

A barbecue: Men in aprons repeatedly squirt quarts of flammable fluid onto chunks of raw meat, creating explosions of flames that shoot high into the air. The explosions continue until the last chunk of meat has turned to cinder.

Lawn care: Seeds are dispersed, then heavy bags of manure, poisonous chemicals, and wood chips are hauled and spread. Shovels, rakes, hoes, assorted hand tools, water sprinklers, and gloves are purchased along with expensive gasoline powered mowing machines. The seeds take root, the grass begins to grow, and it is immediately and systematically chopped down.

Here's another example of pointing out the obvious. Have you ever noticed how awkward, potentially volatile or embarrassing situations are often ignored on purpose? That's usually because nobody knows what to do when they occur. Some people ignore the situation hoping it will disappear, while others try to pretend it doesn't even exist, or make believe it's not as bad as it seems. You can create a funny surprise simply by pointing it out, but you need to be careful. The trick to creating a funny surprise that relieves tension, rather than a shocking surprise that adds to everyone's anxiety is to accurately gauge the level of awareness.

Let's say you're busy hosting a pleasant family gathering when two people begin to argue. Their voices get louder and louder, but none of your guests seem to notice until the argument becomes so intense they take steps to actively ignore it. Their eyes dart around the room looking for a diversion. Some guests get up to leave the room. Others initiate meaningless conversations. Everyone is aware of the conflict, but feels helpless to do anything about it. Now is the time to make your move.

It's a perfect set up for a punch line. Why? Recall how the classic joke works. The audience is surprised by a punch line when they've been sufficiently set up to believe they know what will happen next. Then suddenly, they realize they've been fooled and laughter ensues.

Here the loud argument has made everyone uncomfortable, the party is about to be ruined, and your guests expect the worst. A clever comment pointing out the obvious can relieve tension, and lead everyone in another direction.

Pick up a pad and pencil, then announce: "I score it five rounds for Aunt Mary, and five rounds for Cousin Bill. I guess that makes it a draw. Now, who would like dessert?"

Say Anything Often Enough

Repetition is another tool you can use to amuse. Since we rarely hear the same words or phrases spoken more than twice in succession, you might create a surprise by repeating them more often. Some words are just funnier than others (see below), but repeating any single word over and over again can also sound ridiculous. Try it yourself.

Pick a word, large or small, and say it five or six times in rapid succession.

Politics, politics, politics, politics, politics, politics, politics.

Normally, spoken words communicate meaning, but here the meaning is overshadowed by the repeated vocalizing of the word. The distinction between the word's meaning and its sound becomes blurred. Eventually, much like politics, the listeners will hear only nonsensical noise. This shift into nonsense may itself generate a few laughs, or at least some sympathetic stares.

Are you old enough to remember those early elementary school readers?

See Sally run. Run, Sally. Run! Run! Run!

The repetition sounds childish to adult listeners, so why not make your adult characters speak like children? You'll create an additional surprise and another reason to laugh. Of course the opposite, children repeating adult words, can also be funny:

Behold Sally sprinting. Sprint, Sally. Sprint, I say! Sprint! Sprint! Sprint!

Repetition also focuses a listener's attention, so if you can use the same phrase or word in a variety of new and unexpected ways you might get an extra laugh.

The neighbors think I'm nuts because I hang around this store called The Nut House. I can't stay away from the place. My wife figures I must be nuts about nuts. But she's wrong. It's

not the nuts, it's the bolts.

A related use of repetition is to offer the same response to a variety of statements. Here person A climbs a ladder held by his best friend, person B.

    A: I'm climbing too high.

    B: You'll be fine.

    A: But what if I fall? I could get killed!

    B: You'll be fine.

    A: And my beautiful wife. She'll be so lonely!

    B: I'll be fine.

By and large, language is a tool
for concealing the truth.
George Carlin

Language And Laughter

If you want to think funny, you might follow the example of poets. They know the value of choosing exactly the right word to convey the feeling of a poem. Not just its meaning, but the sound it makes when read aloud, where it's placed in the poem, how it looks on the page, the number of syllables, and where the accents fall.

Precise word choice is especially important to standup comedians where clarity and brevity are key ingredients, but anyone trying to be funny can employ the power of poetry. Techniques like alliteration ("employ the power of poetry"), rhyming, and the rhythmic flow of words or ideas can draw attention to your work.

Many words and phrases in the English language can only be understood within the context in which they are used. Consider colloquial expressions, the specialized vocabularies of many professions, as well as the inclusion of assorted foreign words and accents, and you'll begin to understand how the meaning of a word or sentence can change from moment to moment.

Despite such ambiguities and uncertainties we genuinely expect to understand each other, and most of us assume language is governed by a limited set of clearly defined rules. This is great news for humorists. If your audience expects to understand you, they'll be surprised when they don't. Or rather, they'll be surprised when they realize the language you're using means something completely different than what they had expected.

A waiter prepares to take a customer's order.

WAITER: May I help you, Sir?

CUSTOMER: Yes, please. I see there's roast turkey with home-style mashed potatoes and gravy on the menu this evening.

WAITER: I'm terribly sorry, Sir. I'll get you a clean one right away.

Double entendres (a single word or phrase with a double meaning), puns (twisting a word's meaning or sound), spoonerisms (switching the initial sounds of words), tom swifties (the knife thrower remarked pointedly), limericks and malapropisms in general are often funny, but use them

61

judiciously unless clever wordplay is the centerpiece of your work.[1]

I entered ten puns in the comedy writer's contest hoping one might win. But no pun in ten did.

Short words starting with explosive consonants (p, t, b, g, d) or containing hard consonant sounds, particularly a "K" sound ("K" or hard "C" sounds), can be especially humorous. One theory is that "K" words sound like laughter: keh, keh, keh. Notice how words like chicken, duck, and cluck compare to robin, sparrow, and sing. Ask yourself which is funnier: a pair of green trousers, or a pair of pickle pants?

Some words simply look or sound funny all by themselves. You'll have to decide which ones of course, although hippopotamus and drool come immediately to my strange mind along with noodle and blubber. (Blubber, with its three fat b's, even looks like blubber.) Experiment using words that have an unusual spelling and/or pronunciation. They'll add an additional element of surprise and, perhaps, humor.

---

[1] Be aware that some people consider wordplay to be a lower form of humor, and may even be offended or embarrassed by its use. My own view is that humor in any form is best judged in terms of the laughter it produces.

Names of people, places, and things can also be intrinsically funny. For example, writer and director Preston Sturges (A pretty funny name itself. It sounds to me like a fish: the Preston Sturgeon.) populated his 1940s comedy films with people like Trudy Kockenlocker and John D. Hackensacker. Notice the "K" sound in each name.

Whether the words you select are found in a dictionary or created spontaneously, they can be used however you like as long as they add humor. You might even consider speaking double-talk.

There's a thin line between
to laugh with and to laugh at.
Richard Pryor

Double-Talk

One practitioner of double-talk defines it this way: "Double-talk is strictly brannis talk with the caboshen growing out of the seedle fornstaff."[2]

Let me clarify. Double-talk sounds like normal speech, but includes nonsense words to confuse the listener. The listener is first confused, then surprised, and finally amazed and amused to learn the speaker has mastered such verbal artistry.

Some of the basic principles of double-talk include:

1. Keep a straight face. No funny business allowed.

2. Speak with earnestness. Mean what you say.

3. Use nonsense words that sound ordinary: I used a knife to *stim* my *fridnap*.

4. Speak about the subject at hand, rather than a new topic. Don't distract the listener.

---

[2] This quote and much of what follows come from an out of print pamphlet called X-Jargon by Wallace Lee.

5.	Surround the nonsense word with clearly pronounced words. Disguise your intentions.

6.	Use double-talk only among good speakers of English. They'll think they should understand what's been said.

The funniest double-talk sounds like normal, everyday conversation:

> You might walk into a store and say to the clerk, "That dow for a booberday, how much is it?"

> Or you could place an order in a restaurant.
> " I'll have two snibbles and a cup of coffee."

However else you decide to use double-talk, just make sure the freebestan at the end of the needlefuss is kept in an upright position.

Get Physical

Tripping over your own feet, falling down a flight of stairs, bumping into a wall, door or a metal pole, and the immortal pratfall created by slipping on a banana peel are just a few examples of physical humor. Some legendary examples from the last century include Charlie Chaplin's walk, Harpo Marx using his knee to shake hands, and Jerry Lewis running amok. Buster Keaton made an entire career as The Great Stone Face, and Carol Burnett's television characters could always be identified by their physical peculiarities.

Exaggerate or minimize a character's physical appearance or actions and you may create a funny surprise. Think too much hair or too little, overweight or underfed, a pug nose or a giant proboscis. Maybe you or your character is a big man who takes teeny-tiny steps when he walks, or has a squeaky voice. Or, perhaps she's an elegantly dressed woman who can bench press five hundred pounds and do back-flips. Turn your character into a walking, talking contradiction.

You might start by evaluating your own physical appearance. Be brave and take a look in the mirror. Handsome? Beautiful? Of course you are. But consider this: What might happen if you exaggerated or minimized any of

those highly attractive features? Oh, and while you're in front
of the mirror, why not make some funny faces? Go ahead.
Stick out your tongue.

In the end, everything is a gag.
Charlie Chaplin

Sight Gags

Try explaining to someone who hasn't seen them, what's so funny about The Three Stooges. "They slap and punch each other, hit each other with hammers and wooden planks, Moe pulls out Larry's hair and then pokes him in the eyes, and Curly makes this funny noise while he slaps the top of his head." Obviously, sight gags must be seen to be appreciated.

Sight gags have been around ever since the first cave woman smacked her inattentive husband over the head with a rock. Today, clowns are the expert practitioners of sight gags. Face paint, wigs, floppy shoes, pulling a giant bouquet of flowers from a pair of baggy pants, and squirting water from a corsage are all well-known gags that continue to entertain us.

Consider Lucille Ball stuffing chocolates in her mouth on an assembly line, slipping in a vat of crushed grapes, or getting drunk on Vita Veta Vegiman. Those classic gags are still funny even after decades of television re-runs.

Effective sight gags take preparation, physical dexterity, and plenty of practice. You may not have the time or inclination to become an amateur clown, but you can still create funny effects by the way you perform familiar activities.

Why not eat an ice cream cone with a knife and fork, go to work with your clothes on inside-out and backwards, or pay a visit to the local hospital dressed like the Grim Reaper?

Okay, so maybe you don't want to get fired from your job or arrested for being a public nuisance. The point is creating sight gags requires you to think funny. Look around and ask yourself, "What if things were done differently...very differently?" Remember, opportunities to generate laughter are everywhere.

I am thankful for laughter, except when milk
comes out my nose.
Woody Allen

Who's There?

Getting laughs will be easy if you can impersonate a well-known celebrity or public figure. By imitating a person's voice and mannerisms, you can suddenly bring them to life right in front of your audience. What could be more unexpected than that?

The fact that anyone, especially you here and now, would work so hard to impersonate someone else is itself surprising. Successfully pulling off the transformation is amazing! Who are you? Are you you, someone else, or two people at once?

The idea is to create the illusion of being another person. Once you've identified and mastered the essentials (movements, speech patterns, tone of voice and mannerisms), you can add humor by using them to set up additional funny bits of business.

Let's say you've decided to imitate that ever-popular target of mimicry, John Wayne.[3] You've mastered his knock-kneed swagger and distinctive speaking style, and you've

---

[3] See the appendix for more tips on doing impressions.

picked out key bits of well-known movie dialogue an audience might expect to hear. Now, how can you add some humor?

You already know the type of character John Wayne played in the movies: the stereotypically masculine American hero – a two-fisted, hard-drinking, independent cuss with a heart of gold. How might you use what you've learned so far to reverse that perception? Take a moment now to think funny and create some unexpected scenarios.

Maybe your John Wayne carries a hair drier instead of a gun, drinks prune juice instead of whiskey, or is afraid of horses. Does he wear cowboy boots, or ballet slippers? Does he carry a six-shooter, or an umbrella? Keep at it and mighty soon you'll have yourself one funny lookin' impersonation.

Humor is reason gone mad.
Groucho Marx

Nuts

Everything is funnier with monkeys! If you don't believe it, just consider the last time you saw someone dressed in a gorilla suit. (Recent local gorilla sightings include the greeter at a convenience store's grand opening, the window wiper at a charity car wash, and a commuter reading the newspaper on the subway.) Sometimes the most unexpected and extravagantly ludicrous buffoonery is hilarious. Have you ever doubled over with laughter and couldn't stop? Often, nonsensical situations are the trigger. "I don't know why, but I just couldn't stop laughing!" This kind of humor has been called anarchistic, since it doesn't follow any set of rules. Perhaps that's what's so surprising about it.

The most well known practitioners of such shenanigans are the Marx Brothers who, after years performing live on the vaudeville circuit, made their most popular films during The Great Depression. Whenever they suddenly break into a song and dance number, or Harpo pulls out a pair of hedge clippers and snips someone's beard, it's a silly surprise. If you want to join their ranks, you'll need to be prepared to make a fool of yourself at a moment's notice.

Perhaps you could become expert at some nonsensical skill like juggling fresh vegetables, while reciting bawdy limericks. Then, wherever and whenever the impulse strikes, you can leap into action. Sound funny, or just nuts?

Remember, you can always rent that gorilla suit.

I couldn't wait for success, so I went ahead
without it.
Jonathan Winters

The Hot List

If you've read this far, then you've learned quite a bit about the techniques used to create humor. But what about the subject matter? Where do funny ideas come from?

The short answer is: You're in charge and anything is possible. You determine which subjects are fit to be funny. If a topic is important to you, then go ahead and have fun with it. There is nobody who sees the world as you do, so it's up to you to decide what's so funny about any particular situation. Just let your powerful brain go to work. That being said, you'll improve your chances of creating laughter if you choose topics of extreme interest to your audience.

Some subjects do have universal appeal, and are always relevant. Here's my list of the three hottest topics among humans:

#1 SEX
#2 MONEY
#3 HEALTH.

The Number One hottest topic among humans has to be SEX. Discussing relationships, seeking partners and making sense of sexual experiences. It goes without saying – which is my cue to mention it here – the human race would eventually cease to exist without sex. It's a biologically driven necessity, which may explain why we often find it so absurdly funny.

The topic of sex includes anything having to do with love and romance, intimate relationships, masculinity and femininity, marriage and divorce, raising families, and sexual orientation. Each of these general topics include many others.

Masculinity, for example, might cover subjects like surviving puberty, male displays of physical or mental prowess, competitive sports and the warrior mentality.

Love and romance could lead to jokes about making first contact (formerly called dating), courtship rituals, and the search for Mr. or Ms. Right.

Number Two on the list of hot topics is MONEY. Hard as we may try, few of us can survive without it. This topic includes jobs and careers, saving and spending habits, and the daily struggle to obtain wealth.

Who hasn't had a job or tried to get one? Job hunting, getting along with the boss, those crazy co-workers, office intrigue, the toxic workplace environment, pay raises, hirings and firings are all topics begging for laughter.

Topic Number Three on the list is HEALTH. Health, mental and physical, sounds like a serious subject. It is. Without health you and I are both dead. So, what's so funny about health?

Just consider your last physical exam, visit to the hospital, or the current cost of health insurance. (If you are not laughing yet, stop crying and give it a try.) Other health topics include growing older (it happens all the time), interpreting medical research studies, the benefits and side-effects of prescription drugs, preventing illness, the spread of disease, and yes, even death.

Believe it or not, each of these is a potential gold mine for humorous material. Preventing illness, to give just one example, could lead to jokes about exercise programs and the obesity epidemic, fad diets and diet gurus, folk remedies and non-western philosophies, germs and phobias, allergy shots and flu vaccines.

"But what about death?" In my humble opinion it's still One Big Mystery, so the humor field is wide open. But you might start by observing the many ways we humans handle grieving, loss, and the memories of those we loved (or did not love). Consider undertakers and funeral parlors, funeral ceremonies and cemeteries, wills, or cremation versus burial.

Notice that the three hottest topics—sex, money and health—have a lot in common with each other. They're all necessary for human existence, and most of the time you can't have one without influencing another. The next time you watch a stand-up comedian, count the number of jokes about sex, money or health and you'll understand why they're at the top of the hot topics list.

I looked up my family tree
and found out I was the sap.
Rodney Dangerfield

Style Points

Effectively sharing your sense of humor may require more than a hot topic and a strong punch line. It can also involve style; the manner in which you express your funny ideas. Two people can tell the same joke yet, depending on how it was presented, one might create laughter while the other produces silence.

The most important rule governing style is simply to start with yourself. That means getting in touch with your feelings about the topics at hand. If, for example, you're writing a humorous article about a pet peeve, then your anger should be obvious to your readers. If you're telling a funny story about a recent romantic misadventure, then perhaps you'll express a sense of self-mockery. If you're reciting a list of peculiar observations, you may want to do it in a way that reveals the quirky side of your own personality.

You may be shy, suffer from performance anxiety or fear the wrath of an editor's pen, but you should also feel comfortable with what you're saying and how you're saying it. Comfort creates confidence, which in turn will help you connect with your audience.

Style can enhance your sense of humor in a variety of ways. Besides the tone of your spoken or written voice, your style can also be expressed through your physical appearance, facial expressions, and physical movements.

Think of Rodney Dangerfield, a standup comedian who carved out an entire career as the man who got no respect. His apprehensive delivery, bulging eyes, facial ticks, and uncomfortable necktie made him look, act and sound like a man victimized by the whole world. The character is a specific comic creation, but there's no denying it was one that Rodney Dangerfield felt comfortable portraying.[4] His jokes were always well-crafted, but he sold them to his audience with his style.

The best way to discover your own style is to experiment. Exaggerate your emotions, or try to eliminate them completely. Try out a highly animated approach to trivial topics, or use a deadpan delivery to explore controversial subjects. Go to extremes until you begin to locate your comfort zone. You'll find your comic style evolving as you gain experience sharing your sense of humor.

---

[4] Although the consequences were not always to his liking. Ironically, people often treated him in real life like the buffoon he portrayed in his act. It was a problem that continued to haunt him despite his great success.

Putting It All Together

The techniques I've described will help you think funny on a daily basis, but you'll have to continue practicing if you really want to get into the humor habit. Here are seventeen activities to assist you.

1. Start a file, pile or list of your favorite jokes and cartoons. Any time you hear something funny, write it down and add it to your collection. Do the same with cartoons you find on the Internet, in magazines, or the newspaper. Then, set aside some time to review your work. See if you can identify set-up and punch lines, or examples of exaggeration or understatement. Now put yourself in the humorist's shoes and try to imagine the thinking that went into the creation of each joke or cartoon. Finally, try to create your own jokes and/or cartoon ideas based on the same topics.

2. Watch hit TV sitcoms. *Seinfeld* and *The Simpsons* are more recent hits, but you can also learn a lot from oldies like *I Love Lucy*, *All in the Family*, *MASH* or *The Cosby Show*. What makes them so funny season after season, year after year, and re-run after re-run? You can learn a lot by watching, but you can learn even more by studying what

you watch. How are humorous topics introduced? Can you identify examples of exaggeration, physical humor, sight gags, or funny words? Focus on a single character, for example Kramer from *Seinfeld*, and try to identify the behaviors and bits of dialogue that add humor.

3. Watch unfunny TV sitcoms. This exercise sounds painful, but the results may astound you. Pick a sitcom you avoid watching because it isn't funny, and watch it straight through. Now take a deep breath and write down any instances in the show where, instead of laughing, you felt particularly disappointed, embarrassed, anxious, or bored. What caused you to feel this way? Are there instances where the punch lines were predictable, unrelated to the set-ups, or missing entirely? What character behaviors did you find particularly annoying? Were you ever surprised? Exploring why a bad sitcom failed to make you laugh is an effective way to get in touch with your own sense of humor.

4. Enjoy the classics. The American Film Institute polled film industry leaders and then made a list of the top 100 funniest films of all-time (*Some Like It Hot* was number one). Why not rent ten or twenty of them and spend the entire week laughing? You're bound to pick up a few tips.

5. Hang Around the Pros. Visit a comedy club and experience live professional comedians in action. A good second choice is to watch any of the many comedy concert DVDs available. If you're not laughing too hard yourself, try to notice when your favorite performers get the biggest audience responses. What makes those moments funny? Even if you can't come up with any definite answers, the exercise will increase your awareness of what's so funny.

6. Read a joke book. The shelves of libraries and bookstores are full of joke books. Many were written to provide public speakers with instant material. Some focus on a single topic such as romance, growing old, careers, etc., while others contain jokes for every occasion. Pick one or two books and flip through them. Pick out several jokes at random and examine them. What makes them work (or not work)? How might they be improved? Can you write five or six more jokes on the same topic?

7. Reenact the classic routines. Make your own list of favorite comedy bits and try to reenact them. Many film scripts are available on the Internet, and you can transcribe others or simply replay the videotapes, CDs or DVDs for comparison. Have a friend or spouse be Stan Laurel to your Oliver Hardy, Groucho to your Chico, or Bud Abbot

to your Lou Costello. Try to deliver a wisecrack like Bob Hope, or do a take and double take like Jack Benny. Notice how timing, physical movements, tone of voice and facial expressions add humor. Can you identify any signature behaviors? For example, Oliver Hardy often played with his tie. You'll soon develop an appreciation for the effort that went into creating a classic.

8. Read and study humorous essays. *The New Yorker* magazine has a humorous essay (and plenty of cartoons) in every issue. Newspapers usually carry one or two amusing opinion pieces every week, and your local librarian can direct you to entire collections of humorous essays written by some of the country's greatest writers. How does the author create the surprises that make you laugh? Are there any specific comedy techniques you can identify? How would you describe the author's style of writing, and how is it related to the topic of the essay?

9. Listen to the language used in plays and poems. See if you can discover how word choice and rhythm add humor.

10. Sing a funny song. Write humorous new lyrics to a popular or well-known song. How about starting with *Over the Rainbow*? Record it, play it back and make it even funnier.

11. Make a list of boring activities. Trying to turn the mundane into the hilarious is good practice. Activities like washing the dishes, preparing breakfast, getting dressed in the morning, and driving to work are all pretty boring. How might you add some humor to them? Take each activity in your list and apply one or more of the techniques described in the book. Preparing breakfast, for example, offers plenty of opportunities for sight gags. How about a coffee maker that goes berserk, or a loaf of bread that must be sliced with a power saw?

12. Read the standup comedians. Bill Cosby, George Carlin, Jerry Seinfeld, and it seems nearly everyone else who has ever successfully performed standup comedy have written books. Most contain excerpts from their standup routines, and many contain humorous stories about their personal misadventures. Your assignment remains the same: Try to discover what's so funny.

13. Make Monday Pun Day. Spend an entire day using a specific comic technique. Use as many puns as possible on Monday. Turn Tuesday into a day full of exaggerations. Wednesday you can practice minimizing everything that happens. Search for groups of threes on Thursdays.

Friday is a perfect day to use sight gags. Double-talk your way through the shopping mall on Saturday. And on Sunday, well why not do something completely nuts?

14. What's new? The newspaper is full of absurd situations and headline stories just waiting to be ridiculed. Pick one or two articles and try to create some laughs. Stories involving politicians are always good for a chuckle or two. Go through each paragraph and add a bit of humor by exaggerating, using funny words, or completely reversing the action.

15. Embrace your blunders. Errors, accidents, and blunders are part of life. Most of the time they are a surprise. It's hard to laugh when you are the victim but afterwards, when the outcome is clear and there is nothing left to fear, that surprise may seem like a joke. Why not use the experience to hone your humor skills? Let's say you tripped and fell on the stairs going into your apartment. You could easily exaggerate the story by adding an extra flight or two of stairs to fall down, loading your arms with several bags of groceries, and allowing fruits and vegetables to fly through the air when you fell. Your imaginary accident might generate some real guffaws.

16. Fracture a fairy tale. Select a well known fairy tale and make it funny. Since these stories are well known, audiences have definite and clearly defined expectations as to what's going to happen. Your job is to pull the magic carpet out from under them. Change the characters, alter the plot, and/or distort the ending. Use all the comedy tools at your disposal, and then re-tell the tale in its new and improved form.

17. Use idiotic idioms. Make a list of idiomatic expressions, proverbs, aphorisms, mottoes, or otherwise well-known sayings and turn them into something idiotic. See how many variations you can create, and remember to have fun. Don't get bitten by more than you want to chew, or let the task become an albacore around your neck.

The Ultimate Test

Whatever makes you laugh is funny, and anything is funny if it makes you laugh. That's the basic truth about comedy. Remember?

No matter what you do to sharpen your sense of humor, the ultimate test is whether or not the results make you laugh. Monitor yourself as you go along, and keep at it until you are smiling, snickering, giggling, or howling.

You'll soon discover your own humorous sensibility – what you find funny, what makes you laugh and why. Keep practicing and you'll develop an instinct for identifying and creating funny situations.

Soon you'll be spreading laughter at every opportunity. You'll meet new friends. Your love life will improve dramatically, and you will become wealthy beyond your wildest dreams. Well maybe not that entire last part, but I can guarantee you will get more fun out of each day.

Think funny and enjoy life from new perspectives. It's all about breaking with routines, moving away from the status quo, charting new courses, and reversing trends. Above all, thinking funny is about surprises. Inventing them and sharing them.

Nobody sees the world exactly as you see it. Nobody has your special sense of humor. I hope as you discover what's so funny you'll share your views, and offer the rest of us a new vantage point from which to enjoy "this cockeyed caravan".

Appendix

General Tips for Impersonating People

1.　Pick a well-known subject to impersonate, preferably someone of the same sex. If you are putting together a professional act, you will want to avoid cliché impersonations. Jack Nicholson, Jimmy Stewart, John Wayne, Al Pacino, and William Shatner have been done so often audiences are rarely surprised. That's not to say you can't develop a new twist, but as a beginner why make your task more difficult?

2.　Pick someone your audience will recognize. You may do a great imitation of your Aunt Edna, but if nobody knows Aunt Edna besides you and Uncle Ed then he'll be the only one laughing. Likewise, you may be a dedicated sci-fi fan, but will your audience appreciate your impersonation of the robot Gort and your clever references to the classic 1950's film, *The Day The Earth Stood Still*? (Haven't seen it? Klaatu – barada – nikto!)

3.   Pick someone you can study. You'll need to see your subject walk, talk and perform any well-known actions over and over. Unless you know a famous celebrity who loves being observed at close range, you'll need to settle for videotapes, DVDs and/or sound recordings.

4.   Identify the characteristics you want to imitate. What makes this person distinctive? Is it the way he/she talks, walks, moves, or is it something else? Make a list, and be specific. The late Frank Gorshen did over forty different celebrity impressions. His advice: "You had to look like them and walk like them. Once you get that down, the voice comes easy."

5.   Break down the items in your list into manageable bits. Let's say you want to impersonate Jimmy Stewart as he appeared in the film *It's A Wonderful Life,* and you've identified his stuttering speech as one of his defining characteristics. When does he stutter? Is it at the beginning, in the middle, or at the end of a sentence? Does he repeat single words or entire phrases, whole words or only parts of them? Does the volume of his voice increase or decrease when he stutters? Are there any specific mannerisms, like running his hand through his hair, that usually accompany the stuttering?

6.   Identify and gather resource materials like DVDs , photographs and audio or video tapes, you can use over and over again to study each specific characteristic.

7.   Practice. Use mirrors, tape recorders, video cameras, and supportive audience volunteers to compare your impersonation to the real thing. If it's just not working, break it down into smaller pieces: speeches into sentences, sentences into phrases, phrases into words and words into syllables. Do the same thing with physical movements and facial expressions.

8.   Optional: Use props, clothing and theatrical makeup to approximate your subject's physical appearance.

Additional Reading

Here are a few of my favorites. All are recent publications.

Damn! That's Funny! Writing Humor You Can Sell by Gene Perret. (Written by a seasoned professional, this book covers many types of humor writing including monologues, gags, essays, parodies, sketches, and short anecdotes. A practical guide with valuable insights.)

Step By Step To Stand-Up Comedy by Greg Dean. (Explains his proven method for constructing jokes and developing a successful comedy routine.)

Patrick Page's Book of Visual Comedy by Patrick Page. (Clearly explains how and why pratfalls are funny. A how-to book for magicians, clowns, speakers and anyone else looking for fun.)

A Walk In The Woods by Bill Bryson. (A hilarious, best-selling account of his attempt to hike the Appalachian Trail.)

Comic Insights: The Art of Stand-Up Comedy by Franklin Ajaye.(Conversations with more than a dozen of today's top comedians.)

About The Author

Paul Moran is a writer, artist and former
teacher, who taught Special Education
classes for eighteen years. Samples of
Paul's art work can be viewed on the
Internet at www.decoboxes.com. He
and his multitalented wife Linda live in
Fairfax, Virginia.

Glossary

Amuse: (v.) To entertain or cause laughter.

Clown: (n.) A performer who entertains by playing the fool.

Comedian: (n.) A person who amuses others.

Comedy: (n.) A more or less funny story with a non-tragic theme and a happy ending.

Comic: (n.) A comedian. (adj) Anything having to do with comedy.

Funny: (adj.) Anything that excites laughter.

Glossary: (n.) A generally useless listing of common words and simple definitions hidden at the end of a book.

Hilarious: (adj.) Anything that excites loud laughter or merriment.

Humorist: (n.) A skilled writer or teller of funny stories.

Joke: (n.) Anything said or done to arouse laughter.

Laughter: (n.) The sound people make when they are amused.

Sense of Humor: The universal human ability to recognize what's so funny.

Surprise: (n.) The experience of the unexpected.